The Greatest City in Sports
Copyright ©2016 by Daniel J. Schmitt
GCIS Publishing, LLC
All rights reserved.

ISBN 978-0-9976066-2-1

First edition: 2015

Photography consulting and optimization courtesy of John Sommers.

Design services provided by Hill Harcourt, Ashton Advertising.

Printed in the United States through Four Colour Print Group.

All proprietary names, images, or other intellectual property are trademarks or registered trademarks of their respective holders. Usage of them in this book does not imply any endorsement by or affiliation with them.

For preorders, bulk purchasing discounts, and customized design please contact us at greatestcityinsports@gmail.com

Contents

- ⚜ Muhammad Ali 8
- ⚜ The Kentucky Derby 14
- ⚜ Louisville Slugger 20
- ⚜ Johnny Unitas 26
- ⚜ University of Louisville 30
- ⚜ The Greatest Rivalry 38
- ⚜ The Greatest Fans 46
- ⚜ Valhalla Golf Club 54
- ⚜ Amateurs, Pros, and Nicknames 60
- ⚜ Flashes of Greatness 66

The fleur de lis emblem featured throughout this book (and prominently on the back cover) is a popular symbol of Louisville, widely displayed on storefronts and bumper stickers around town. It pays homage to King Louis XVI, after whom Louisville was named, and serves as a common source of pride and unity. Hopefully, this book will do the same.

Quick, sports fans…

Quick, sports fans, name the one athlete that comes to mind when you hear these two words: "The Greatest."
Any true sports fan knows that of all the captivating figures in the history of sport, The Greatest is, of course, Muhammad Ali. Michael Jordan was "Air Jordan," Wayne Gretzky was "The Great One," George Herman Ruth was "The Babe," but The Greatest was Muhammad Ali – The Louisville Lip. Even though Ali did not win or defend any of his three heavyweight boxing championships in Louisville, Cassius Clay (as we first knew him) was born and raised here and is still considered Louisville's favorite son.

Now I know that declaring Louisville to be the greatest city in sports is quite bold, and maybe even a bit surprising, but having a significant attachment to a consensus top five athlete of all time (#2 on ESPN's Sports Century list of greatest athletes) has to at least put us in the conversation. Notice I said "us." I am a Louisvillian and admittedly biased.

OK, nice book, but get real. Do you really think Louisville, KY is the greatest city in sports? What about New York City, Los Angeles, Chicago, Pittsburgh, Boston, Atlanta, or twenty other major cities that dwarf Louisville in size, population, money, etc? Well, quite simply, yes I do.

Take any other city and answer these questions:

- Who is that city's favorite son? Greater than Muhammad Ali?
- What is that city's most prolific annual sporting event? Greater than the Kentucky Derby - "The greatest two minutes in sports?"
- What is that city's most recognizable sports brand? Greater than Louisville Slugger?
- What is that city's most heated rivalry, and how passionate are the fans? Greater than UofL vs UK?
- Oh, and the man who is often called the greatest quarterback of all time, the man who engineered the game winning drive in what is commonly referred to as 'the greatest game ever played' (1958 NFL Championship) – Johnny Unitas – played his college football at the University of Louisville. We knew his greatness before the rest of the world…

These questions are just the beginning. And, yes, many cities have very good answers to those questions posed above. A few have excellent answers. Boston, for example, could bring up Larry Bird, the Boston Marathon, Boston Garden, the Red Sox, Bruins, etc. They try to throw in the Patriots, but Foxborough is actually closer to Providence than Boston. Either way, is that greater than Muhammad Ali, the Kentucky Derby, Louisville Slugger, Johnny Unitas, etc? It really is debatable. And that is the point.
Oh, and Bird is not from Boston by the way. He is from French Lick, IN, which is much closer to Louisville, KY.

Ali, on the other hand, is ours – all ours. After he won his second heavyweight title by upsetting the previously undefeated George Foreman, he made a point immediately after the fight to say, *"Hello to all my friends in Louisville, KY…I'm recognized all over the world now, but my greatness came and started in Louisville, KY…<u>Louisville is the greatest! Louisville is the greatest!</u>"*

About the Author

Well, I am probably a lot like you. I was born here, I live here, and I love it here. I have always felt like the sports landscape in our city was not only great, but uniquely great - and that we should somehow harness it.

I truly enjoyed my extensive research for this project, but I am just a fan, not an expert. I have had this idea in my head for as long as I can remember, but I just never acted on it until I happened to watch a replay of the first Ali-Frazier fight a few years ago.

Have you ever watched that fight?

If you are a sports fan - from any city, but especially from Louisville, KY – and you have never studied the career of Muhammad Ali, do yourself a favor and watch that first Ali-Frazier fight from March 8th, 1971. The two men were a combined 57-0 entering the bout, and it was billed as "The Fight of the Century." They did not disappoint.

Many wonderful books have been written that go into great detail about Ali and these other truly great sports figures. The aim of this book is to just give some highlights…to give the reader just enough to inspire you to do your own research on this amazing city…and to make the case for Louisville as *The Greatest* City in Sports.

One Day in Louisville…

So one summer day, I finally decided to do something with this idea by taking in as many Louisville landmarks and museums as possible. I visited Valhalla Golf Club and the campus and athletic facilities at the University of Louisville. I felt the chills tingle down my spine from the mesmerizing 360° movie theatre showing of "The Greatest Race" at the Kentucky Derby Museum, toured Churchill Downs, and learned that a 1200-lb thoroughbred can reach top speeds of 40+ mph in only 3 strides. I stared down the barrel of the largest bat in the world, marveled at what baseball's brightest stars accomplished with a Louisville Slugger in their hands, and stood in the batter's box for a 90-mph fastball. And, of course, I visited my favorite spot in all of Louisville – The Ali Center.

I even had time to stop in for lunch with my 93-year-old grandma at her house in Butchertown where she has lived for well over 50 years. I have no way of proving this, but she is the greatest cook in the world. Don't be surprised – she is from Louisville. Others might disagree with this claim, just like they might disagree with the bold claim of this book, but both are absolutely true to me, and I cannot be convinced otherwise. Maybe her cooking wouldn't taste the same if not enjoyed in her kitchen, in her company, at the very table where my grandpa used to sit. And maybe Louisville's greatness is not only about those people who have done great things here – but also about the people who embrace them, cheer for them, and love them.

Muhammad Ali

- Born January 17th, 1942 in Louisville, KY.
- Won his professional boxing **debut in Louisville's Freedom Hall** on October 29th, 1960.
- Won his first 31 professional fights (10/29/60 – 12/7/70) before losing to Joe Frazier in a 15-round unanimous decision on March 8th, 1971. **He later beat Joe Frazier twice.**
- Won his next ten fights (7/26/71 - 2/14/73) before losing to Ken Norton in a 12-round split decision on March 31st, 1973. **He later beat Ken Norton twice.**
- Won his next 14 fights before losing to Leon Spinks in a 15-round split decision on February 15th, 1978. **He beat Leon Spinks 7 months later** by Unanimous Decision.
- So in his first 18 years of professional boxing, Ali was 56-3, and he **avenged each loss** by beating Joe Frazier twice, Ken Norton twice, and Leon Spinks once – leaving no doubt who was, indeed, *The Greatest*.
- All-Time Record: 56-5, 37 knockouts.
- **Ali was never knocked out.**

Muhammad Ali

- Won the **gold medal** in Light Heavyweight Boxing in 1960 at the Rome Olympics.

- Won the World Heavyweight Boxing Championship vs. Sonny Liston (35-1) in 1964 **as a 7-1 underdog**.

- Won the World Heavyweight Boxing Championship vs. George Foreman (40-0) in 1974 **as a 3-1 underdog**.

- Won the World Heavyweight Boxing Championship vs. Leon Spinks (7-0) in 1978, to become **the only three-time champ in history**.

- Has appeared on the cover of Sports Illustrated 39 times and named **Sportsman of the Century** by S.I. in 1999.

Heavyweight Boxing Champions from Louisville, KY

⚜ **Jimmy Ellis: 40-12-1 (24 KO)**
When Ali was stripped of the world title for draft evasion (which was eventually overturned in the Supreme Court by unanimous decision), the World Boxing Association staged an 8-man tournament for the belt. Ellis was ranked #8 in the world and was the betting underdog in all three fights, but he won all three and became the second consecutive WBA heavyweight champion from Louisville, KY on 04/27/68.

⚜ **Greg Page: 58-17-1 (48 KO)**
Born in Louisville, KY and won the World Heavyweight Boxing Title on 01/12/84 vs. Gerrie "The Bionic Hand" Coetzee via 8th round Knock-Out.

Thus, since the World Boxing Association was formed in 1921, three of the forty-three heavyweight champions were born in Louisville, KY…the birthplace of greatness.

⚜ Also, **Marvin Hart (aka "The Louisville Plumber")** won the World Heavyweight Boxing Championship against top-ranked Jack Root in 1905 (pre-WBA), and also beat future champion Jack Johnson that same year.

The Kentucky Derby

- "The Greatest Two Minutes in Sports"
- "The Fastest Two Minutes in Sports"
- "The Most Exciting Two Minutes in Sports"
- "The Run For The Roses"
- Run every year since 1875 in Louisville, KY – making it the longest-running annual sporting event of any kind in the United States.
- Attendance has exceeded 150,000 over a dozen times, with a record crowd of 170,513 in 2015. That number exceeds the average attendance per game in the NFL, NBA, MLB, and NHL combined.
- Has been attended by US presidents, the Queen of England, and other top dignitaries and celebrities from the world of politics, movies, music, and sports.
- Thunder Over Louisville is the largest annual fireworks display in North America that kicks off a two-week festival of events leading up to race day on the first Saturday in May.
- 2013 Derby Betting at Churchill Downs: $130 Million
- 2013 Super Bowl Betting in Las Vegas Casinos: $99 Million
- 30% more betting, decided in two minutes.

The Kentucky Derby
Fun Facts Every Derby Fan Should Know

- Run every year for 140+ consecutive years at Churchill Downs in Louisville, KY.
- Three-year-old Thoroughbreds race ten furlongs (1.25 miles).
- One of the only races in America which allows up to 20 horses in a single race.
- Only two horses have ever officially finished in less than two minutes: Secretariat (1973) and Monarchos (2001).
- It is speculated that Sham, the runner-up to Secretariat in 1973 may have also beaten two minutes – giving him one of the three fastest times of over 2,000 horses in Derby history, and a second-place finish.
- Secretariat was #35 on ESPNs Sports Century ranking of the top 50 athletes of the 20th century.
- Three fillies (female horses) have won: Regret (1915), Genuine Risk (1980), and Winning Colors (1988).
- Nine geldings (castrated males) have won: most recently, Mine That Bird (2009, 50:1).
- Longshots: Ten horses have won The Derby with odds higher than 23:1, led by Donerail in 1913 at 91-to-1!
- Biggest Payout: In 2005, a $2.00 Superfecta bet on Giacomo, Closing Argument, Afleet Alex, and Don't Get Mad (in order) paid $864,253.50

The Kentucky Derby
The First Jewel of the Triple Crown

- ⚜ The Triple Crown of Thoroughbred Racing consists of a grueling three races in five weeks of varying distances for three-year-old thoroughbreds only:
    - ✓ The Kentucky Derby at Churchill Downs in Louisville, KY (1 ¼ mile).
    - ✓ The Preakness Stakes at Pimlico Race Course in Baltimore, MD (1 3/16 mile).
    - ✓ The Belmont Stakes at Belmont Park in Elmont, NY (1 ½ mile).
- ⚜ The Triple Crown is considered one of the most difficult feats in all of sports due to the age of the horses, the short turnaround between races, and the changing distances.
- ⚜ Only twelve horses have ever won the Triple Crown:

Sir Barton:	1919	**Assault:**	1946
Gallant Fox:	1930	**Citation:**	1948
Omaha:	1935	**Secretariat:**	1973
War Admiral:	1937	**Seattle Slew:**	1977
Whirlaway:	1941	**Affirmed:**	1978
Count Fleet:	1943	**American Pharoah:**	2015

Louisville Slugger

⚜ In 1884, Louisvillian Bud Hillerich was 17 years old and taking the afternoon off from his family's woodworking shop to watch the Louisville Eclipse play baseball. After witnessing his favorite player break a bat during the game, Hillerich offered to make him a new one. That player was fellow Louisville native Pete Browning, who holds the 13th-highest career batting average in Major League Baseball history (.341). Browning's nickname was "the Louisville Slugger."

⚜ Ten years later, in 1894, Bud Hillerich registered the trademark name for his creation: Louisville Slugger.

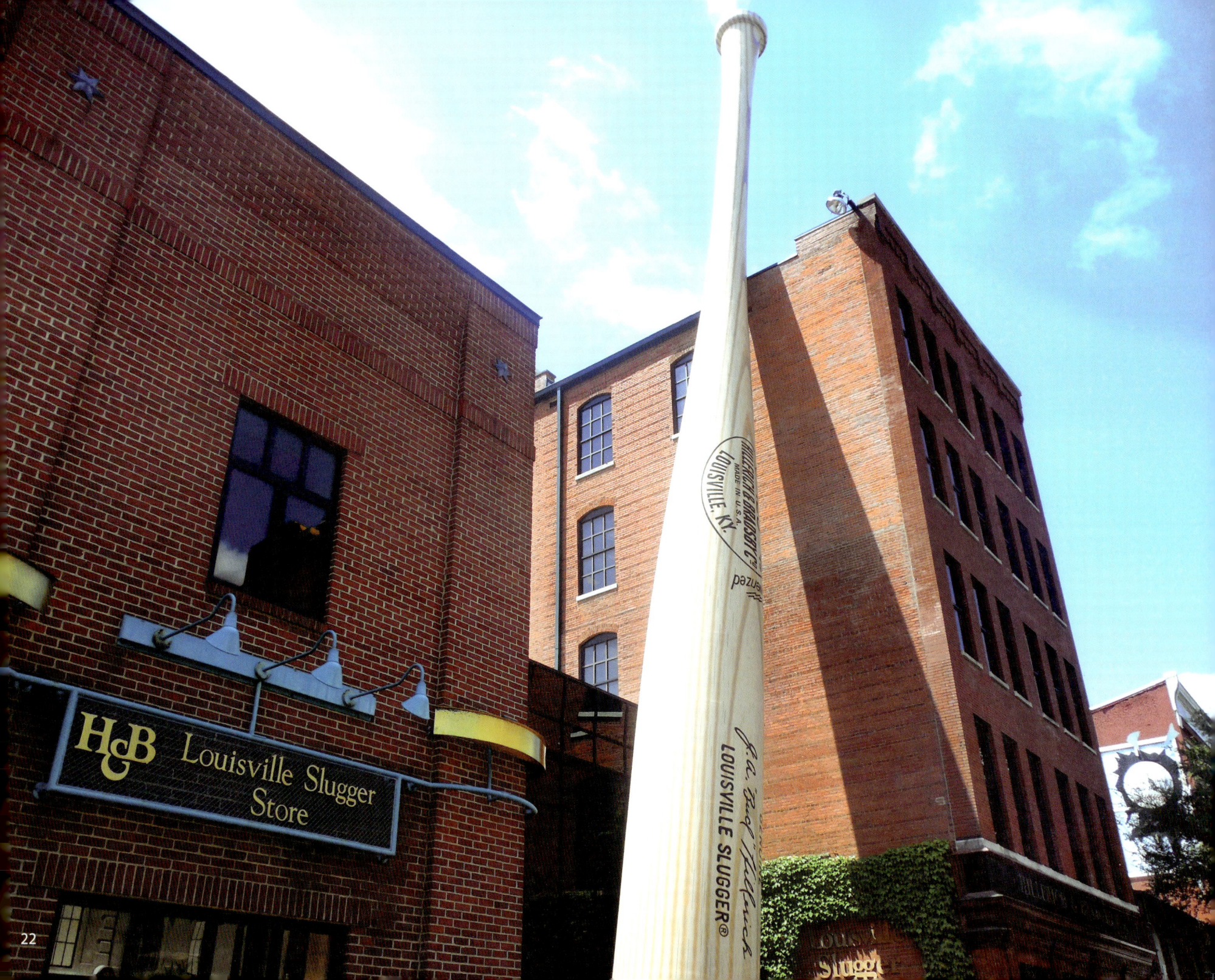

Slugging to Greatness
Blazing a new trail in sports marketing

- Long before Nike, Reebok, Adidas, or Under Armour began signing superstar athletes to endorsement contracts worth millions of dollars, **Louisville Slugger pioneered the practice** of signing endorsement contracts with major league baseball's biggest stars.

- Honus Wagner – who **began his Major League Baseball career with the Louisville Colonels** in 1897 - became the first professional athlete ever to endorse an athletic product by allowing Louisville Slugger to use his name and signature on the barrel of his own bats, and on those sold to the general public in 1905.

- Wagner is still considered by many to be the **greatest shortstop in the history of the game**, and he was elected as one of the first five members in the Baseball Hall of Fame, receiving exactly the same number of votes as Babe Ruth.

- The T206 Honus Wagner baseball card is the **most valuable sports card in history**, with only 50-200 ever printed. Early in production, Wagner refused to allow the American Tobacco Company to continue making his card and selling them in packs of cigarettes. One such card reportedly sold for $2.8 million in 2006.

Louisville Slugger Walk of Fame

One of downtown Louisville's best kept secrets, the Louisville Slugger Walk of Fame stretches from the Louisville Slugger Museum to Louisville Slugger Field, with a bronze caste of each player's bat and a summary of career highlights engraved onto home plate. These monuments are interspersed down the sidewalk of Main Street, reminding fans of the **greatest accomplishments in baseball history – and their unique connection to Louisville**. Each and every player enshrined was under contract with Louisville Slugger. Here is a small sampling of some of their most remarkable achievements, with all-time rank in parentheses:

- Hank Aaron: 755 Career HRs (#1)*
- Ty Cobb: .367 Career Batting Avg. (#1)
- Joe DiMaggio: 56-game hitting streak in 1941 (#1)
- Lou Gehrig: 3 of top 6 Single-Season RBI Totals (174 in '30, 175 in '27, 184 in '31)
- Mickey Mantle: 18 Career World Series HRs (#1)
- Roger Maris: 61 HRs in 1961 (#1)*
- Stan Musial: 24 All-Star Games (T-#1)
- Cal Ripken, Jr: 2,632 consecutive games played (#1)
- Jackie Robinson: First African American player in the major leagues in 1947, and first professional athlete in any sport to have his jersey number (42) retired universally by every single team.
- Hack Wilson: 191 RBI in 1930 (#1)
- Pete Rose: 4,256 Career Hits (#1)
- Babe Ruth: .690 Career Slugging % (#1)
- Tris Speaker: 792 Career Doubles (#1)
- Honus Wagner: Led the National League in batting average 8 times (T-#1)
- Ted Williams: .482 Career On-Base % (#1) and the last man to bat .400 in a season (.406 in 1941) – only three players have hit over .380 since then: Tony Gwynn (.394 in 1994), George Brett (.390 in 1980), and Rod Carew (.388 in 1977). All three endorsed Louisville Slugger. Often referred to as the greatest hitter in history, Williams said, "I'd have been a .290 hitter without Louisville Slugger."

Johnny Unitas

- University of Louisville Quarterback from 1951-1954.

- Reported to freshman practice weighing 145 pounds.

- Almost transferred to Indiana University after his sophomore season, when 15 teammates were dismissed from school, but **chose to remain a Louisville Cardinal**.

- Threw 27 career Touchdown passes at UofL and was drafted by the Pittsburgh Steelers in 1955.

- A life-sized statue of Unitas overlooks the playing field outside the 2000-square-foot Johnny Unitas Football Museum in Papa John's Cardinal Stadium.

- His #16 jersey is the **only number retired by UofL football**.

- Was presented into the 1979 Pro Football Hall of Fame by Frank Gitschier, **his QB Coach at UofL**.

JOHNNY UNITAS

University of Louisville
Quarterback 1951 - 54

Baltimore Colts 1956 - 1974

Pro Football
Hall of Fame 1979

Johnny Unitas: "The Golden Arm"
Records held as of his retirement after the 1973 season:

- ⚜ #1 in Career Touchdown Passes: 290
- ⚜ #1 in Career Yards Gained: 40,239
- ⚜ #1 in Career Pass Completions: 2,830
- ⚜ #1 in Career Pass Attempts: 5,186
- ⚜ #1 in Career Wins by a starting QB: 118
- ⚜ 47 Consecutive Games with a TD Pass: Record stood for 52 years (broken by Drew Brees in 2012, but Brees threw 844 more passes during his streak: 2,142 vs 1,298).

- ⚜ 3-Time NFL Champion
- ⚜ 3-Time NFL MVP
- ⚜ 10-Time Pro Bowler
- ⚜ Ranked #32 on ESPN SportsCentury's 1999 List of The 50 Greatest Athletes of the 20th Century (6th football player, 2nd quarterback, after only Joe Montana).
- ⚜ Ranked #1 on The Sporting News 2004 list of The 50 Greatest Quarterbacks of All Time (ahead of Montana).

UofL: Men's Basketball

- ⚜ Only program to have won all three major national post-season tournaments:
    - ✓ NAIA Champions in 1948
    - ✓ NIT Champions in 1956
    - ✓ NCAA Champions in 1980, 1986, 2013
- ⚜ 3 NCAA Titles ranks 7th in the nation.
- ⚜ 10 NCAA Final Fours ranks 7th in the nation.
- ⚜ 67 players in the 1,000-Point Career club ranks 2nd.
- ⚜ Two consecutive Hall of Fame coaches:

    Denny Crum (1970-2001) and Rick Pitino (2001-Present) makes 45 years and counting…

UofL: Football
"A collision course with a National Championship..."

- 2007 FedEx Orange Bowl Champs:
  #5 UofL defeated #15 Wake Forest, 24-13

- 2013 AllState Sugar Bowl Champs:
  #22 UofL defeated #4 Florida, 33-23

- In the 16-year existence of the Bowl Championship Series, less than 20 teams won multiple BCS games. Of those that won multiple BCS games, only 5 were undefeated in their BCS appearances. Of those 5 teams that went undefeated, only 2 teams won both games by double digits: The University of Utah and The University of Louisville.

- UofL is the only college football program in America that owns bowl game victories over Alabama (1990 Fiesta Bowl), Florida (2013 Sugar Bowl), and Miami (2013 Russell Athletic Bowl). The Cards outscored these three traditional powers by a combined score of 103-39.

UofL: Year of the Cardinals

In 2012-2013, the University of Louisville became the first and only university in history to win a BCS Bowl Game and reach the Men's Basketball Final Four, the Women's Basketball Final Four, and the College Baseball World Series in the same sports year.

Now that is undeniable greatness.

UofL: Individual Greatness

⚜ Pervis Ellison in 1989 and Angel McCoughtry in 2009 make UofL one of only 4 schools to have ever produced a **#1 Draft Pick** in the NBA and WNBA.

⚜ UofL is one of only two schools to have ever produced an **NFL MVP** (Johnny Unitas), a **Super Bowl MVP** (Deion Branch), and an **NBA MVP** (Wes Unseld).

⚜ Thus, UofL is the **only school in the country** to have a former player in each one of those five prestigious categories.

✓ NFL Most Valuable Player: Johnny Unitas (1959, 1964, 1967)
✓ NBA Most Valuable Player: Wes Unseld (1969)
✓ NBA #1 Draft Pick: Pervis Ellison (1989)
✓ Super Bowl Most Valuable Player: Deion Branch (2005)
✓ WNBA #1 Draft Pick: Angel McCoughtry (2009)

C-A-R-D-S!!!

The Doctors of Dunk **The Dream Game**

The Greatest

Unbreakable IN **ACC**
Fight! U of L **Schnellenberger**
L1C4 **Rick**

U of L

Denny Crum Court **Freedom Hall**
#2 in 1,000-Point Careers **Jim Patterson Stadium**
#3 in Home Attendance **The KFC YUM! Center**
Miracle on Main **Papa Johns Cardinal Stadium**

"They won't play…Well, that's typical."

C-A-T-S!!!

The Governor's Cup **The Fabulous Five**

Rivalry
Sports

SEC **Unforgettable**
Bear Bryant **On, On! U of K**
Pitino **UK2K**

U of K

Memorial Coliseum **Cawood's Court**
Cliff Hagan Stadium **#4 in 1,000-Point Careers**
Rupp Arena **#1 in Home Attendance**
Commonwealth Stadium **Mardis Gras Miracle**

"They don't want to beat us. They want to be us."

The Greatest Rivalry:
University of Louisville vs. University of Kentucky

- ⚜ Ok, Ok, we get it: There are heated rivalries everywhere. There are plenty of fan bases across the world who think their own particular rivalry is the most heated one in all of sports. In a way, rivalry is the essence of sports. There can only be winners if there are losers – and the more it hurts to lose, the better it feels to win. So trust me when I say that losing in this rivalry <u>really</u> hurts. These two universities are located only 75 miles apart in a state without a single professional sports franchise. These two programs get all the attention, all the love, hate, and vitriol – and all the money. A quick look at the statistics on revenue, attendance, and television ratings makes it crystal clear that this rivalry is different. The fans study, work, and live among each other in the same schools, employers, and homes – and are therefore forced to deal with each other on a daily basis. Contrast that to the #2 rivalry on Bleacher Report's 2012 ranking of the most heated rivalries in sports: Ohio State vs. Michigan. That is a tremendous rivalry, for sure, but Columbus, OH and Ann Arbor, MI are over 300 miles apart and each state also hosts teams from the NFL, NBA, MLB, and NHL. With all due respect, it's just not the same.

- ⚜ Oh, and the #1 rivalry on that list is (rightfully) Ali-Frazier, so even if you dispute the greatness of UofL/UK as a rivalry, Louisville wins this category either way.

UofL/UK: Modern-Era Basketball

- Since the NCAA Basketball tournament began in 1939, 11 of the 76 titles preceding the 2015 tourney were won by either UK (8) or UofL (3). Only one state – California (with a population 8x more than KY) – is home to more titles.

- In fact, 5 states: California (15), Kentucky (11), North Carolina (11), Indiana (5), and Connecticut (4) account for 64% of the first 76 NCAA titles.

- But 76 years is a long time, and the game has changed dramatically, so what about the modern era?

- Most experts say the "modern era" of college basketball began with the 1979 title game in which Magic Johnson's Michigan State Spartans defeated Larry Bird's Indiana State Sycamores in what remains the highest-rated college basketball game ever. Interestingly enough, UK won its 5th title the year before (1978) and UofL won its first title the year after (1980), so both universities have won three titles by that definition of "modern era."

- Or, we could mark the "modern era" by introduction of certain rules that make the game "modern," such as:

- 1951 – Tournament expansion to 16 teams.

- 1972 – Freshmen allowed to play varsity.

- 1975 – Tournament expansion to 32 teams. Prior to 1975, only one team per conference could make the NCAA tournament. This often led to many of the country's best teams not participating/ineligible for the tournament.

- 1976 – Elimination of the No-Dunk Rule, for good.

- 1985 – Introduction of the 45-second shot clock.

- 1985 – Tournament expansion to 64 teams.

- 1986 – Introduction of the 3-point line.

- 1993 – Shot clock reduced to 35 seconds.

- 2015 – Shot clock reduced to 30 seconds.

40-Year Modern-Era Basketball Rivalry:
1974/75 – 2013/14

⚜ For this rivalry, in all fairness, it appears that 1975 is the most relevant date to mark the beginning of the "modern era." The tournament had just expanded to 32 teams and UCLA had just finished up an unparalleled run of domination in college basketball by winning ten titles from 1964-1975, beating both UofL and UK in the 1975 Final Four. Since UCLA's dynasty ended with John Wooden's retirement, it is no coincidence that the four most successful programs in the country make up the two fiercest rivalries in college basketball: Duke-North Carolina and Louisville-Kentucky. Familiarity breeds contempt, and rivalry breeds greatness!

⚜ NCAA Tournament Appearances:
UK=34, UofL=32

⚜ Sweet Sixteen Appearances:
UK=24, UofL=21

⚜ Final Four Appearances:
UK=10, UofL=8

⚜ NCAA Championships:
UK=4, UofL=3

⚜ In these 40 years, only 4 schools have made at least 8 Final Fours and won at least 3 National titles:
UNC (12 Final Fours + 4 National Championships)
Duke (12 Final Fours + 4 National Championships)
UK (10 Final Fours + 4 National Championships)
UofL (8 Final Fours + 3 National Championships)

40-Year Overall Rivalry
1974/75 – 2013/14

⚜ Men's Basketball: UK leads the series 24-12, leads in Sweet Sixteens 24-21, leads in Final Fours 11-8, and leads in National Championships 4-3.

⚜ Football: UofL leads the series 13-8, leads in Conference Championships (6-1), leads in Bowl Game Appearances (17-11), and leads in BCS Wins (2-0).

⚜ Women's Basketball: UK leads the series 33-18, but UofL leads in Conference Championships (6-1) and Final Four Appearances (2-0).

⚜ Baseball: UK leads the series 60-25, but UofL leads in Conference Championships (8-1) and College World Series Appearances (3-0).

⚜ So both universities (and fan bases) have their talking points. The pendulum of momentum is bound to swing back and forth over time, but whether you look 40 years in the past or 40 years into the future, this rivalry will stand the test of time in its own special brand of greatness.

All Tied Up!

- ⚜ The University of Kentucky has arguably the greatest tradition in all of college basketball and the University of Louisville has unmistakably solidified itself as a dominant national force. This dynamic captures the pinnacle of true rivalry: A proud, traditional power versus a tenacious and unrelenting challenger, both capable of winning it all in a given year, and whose mere presence infuriates and elevates one another. This intense basketball rivalry has now spilled over into every other sport, many of which have seen UofL pass up "Big Brother" in recent years.

- ⚜ UK has won 8 NCAA men's basketball championships and UofL has won 3. Only six other programs in history have won at least three, and only one (UCLA) has won more than UK's 8. But let's be clear about one thing:

    Ever since Muhammad Ali won the World Heavyweight Boxing title for an unprecedented third time on 9/15/78…

    Ever since Magic and Bird captivated America in the 1979 NCAA title game on 3/26/79…

    Ever since the dawn of ESPN as the world's first 24-hour sports network on 9/7/79…

- ⚜ In the metric that matters most - NCAA Championships - this rivalry is all tied up!

Thank you, UK!

⚜ So will all of you Cardinal fans just say it out-loud with me: *"The University of Kentucky has won eight NCAA men's basketball championships and we may never catch up to that number. One of the reasons we are great is because of them. Thank you, UK."*

Thank you, UofL!

⚜ And will all of you Wildcat fans just say it out-loud with me: *"The University of Louisville has won just as many NCAA men's basketball championships as us over the past 35+ years. One of the reasons we remain great is because of them. Thank you, UofL."*

(Just kidding, everybody. I know that will never happen. However, we should all remember that most of us are far more alike than we are different and hopefully agree that the combined passion for our respective teams is truly without rival. We all make up the greatest rivalry in sports.)

The Greatest Fans

Once again, this category is debatable. That's kind of the point of this whole exercise, right? Every city would like to think they have the best fans in America. Fan is, after all, short for fanatic. The very definition of the word implies a loss of rational thought. It sure would be nice if there was an unbiased third-party organization with high credibility that could somehow quantify just how "fanatical" we all are. Oh wait, there already is. Look no further than the prestigious business school at Emory University in Atlanta, Georgia. On July 15th, 2014 Emory Sports Marketing Analytics published its 2014 College Basketball Fan Equity Rankings aimed at measuring and ranking "college basketball fan support." The authors of this study "create a statistical model of revenue as a function of team quality and market potential and then compare the model's prediction to the self-reported revenues."

If it sounds complicated, it is. But how do we measure fandom, otherwise? I have no idea, but I know the folks at Emory University are far smarter than I ever hope to be. Also, they appear to be unbiased. So, without further ado, here are their 2014 College Basketball Fan Equity Rankings:

1. Louisville
2. Duke
3. Arizona
4. Texas
5. Xavier
6. Syracuse
7. Kentucky
8. Arkansas
9. Oklahoma St.
10. Pittsburgh

Yes, but Louisville won the NCAA Championship in 2013, so of course they would rank very high in 2014, you might say. Actually, massive on-court success makes it statistically more difficult to rank high in this analysis – which makes UofL fans' #1 ranking even that much more impressive. Also, just look back at the prior year's analysis (03/27/13) which was published before Louisville won its first NCAA title in 27 years: UofL's fans were ranked first that year, as well. So with or without the most recent national championship, Louisville college basketball fans are scientifically proven to be the greatest in the sport.

The Greatest Fans

- In 2012, UofL was the #1 revenue-producing Men's College Basketball program in the nation – 64% higher than #2 Syracuse.

- In fact, only 21 *College Football* programs earned more than UofL's massive $42.4 million on men's CBB.

- In 2014, UofL was the only basketball program in the nation to average more than 30,000 combined fans per game for men's and women's home games.

- It was the fourth straight year the Cards exceeded that attendance plateau.

The Greatest in College Basketball

- Entering the 2015 tournament, there have been 76 Division I Champs, 58 Division II Champs, and 78 NAIA Champs.

- The state of Kentucky is home to more combined titles than any other state: UK (8 in D1), UofL (3 in D1), Kentucky Wesleyan (8 in D2), Bellarmine (1 in D2), Kentucky State (3 in NAIA), Georgetown College (2 in NAIA), Pikeville (1 in NAIA), and UofL (1 in NAIA).

- Louisville has also been the host city for 12 NCAA Championship games (Six D1 and Six D2) – more than any other city that has hosted at least one of each.

- Only 9 states are home to a winner in all three postseason tournaments.

- In those 9 states, only one city is home to a champion in all three: Louisville, KY
  - ✓ UofL in Division-1 (1980, 1986, 2013)
  - ✓ Bellarmine in Division-2 (2011)
  - ✓ UofL in NAIA (1948)

- Facts are facts, the city of Louisville and the state of Kentucky are clearly the greatest in college hoops.

Valhalla Golf Club

- Valhalla is the first PGA-owned championship site (purchased from the Gahm family from 1993-2000).

- Valhalla was designed by Jack Nicklaus, who won 18 career Major Championships, and is widely regarded as the greatest golfer ever.

- The statue on the left shows Valhalla founder Dwight Gahm with designer Jack Nicklaus. Its inscription reads: "This is Valhalla, where dreams come true and legends are made."

- Valhalla has hosted 3 PGA Championships, 2 Senior PGA Championships, and the 2008 Ryder Cup – the only US victory in this millennium.

Valhalla Drama

- ⚜ In the 1996 PGA Championship, Mark Brooks defeated Kentuckian Kenny Perry in a sudden-death playoff.

- ⚜ In the 2000 PGA Championship, Tiger Woods defeated Bob May in a three-hole playoff, securing his fifth Major victory.

- ⚜ In the 2014 PGA Championship, Rory McIlroy won his fourth Major by defeating Phil Mickelson by one stroke.

Valhalla Magic

- ⚜ The Ryder Cup is quite possibly the coolest event in professional golf. It features a team of the twelve best American golfers competing against a team of the twelve best European golfers in a three-day match play format. Departing from the traditional golfing format of individuals all competing against the field, the Ryder Cup integrates various one-on-one and two-on-two golf competitions to accumulate points for the overall team/country. Each Ryder Cup consists of 28 matches with the winning team getting one point and each team getting ½ point for a tie. Thus, it requires 14.5 points or more to win the event.

- ⚜ This prestigious competition is held every two years, with the host site alternating between the finest courses in the United States and Europe.

- ⚜ The golfers are not paid anything for this event.

- ⚜ The United States initially dominated Ryder Cup play – winning 19 of 22 times - when it was only the US vs. Great Britain (1927-1971) and later the US vs. Great Britain + Ireland (1973-1977).

- ⚜ However, the US has won only 7 of 18 modern day Ryder Cups since the format changed to allow golfers from the entire continent of Europe to compete against the US team. And since the turn of the century, the European team is undefeated, outscoring Team USA by a combined point total of 98-70, *except for the 2008 Ryder Cup at Valhalla Golf Club in Louisville, KY.*

Amateur to Professional Greatness

- In 2002, Louisville Valley Sports American Little League **won the Little League World Series**.
- In the early years of the Little League World Series (1947-1966) 18 of the first 20 champions were from the US, but since 1967, teams from outside the US have won 32 of the 47 titles.
- Valley Sports went **undefeated** on their road to the LLWS, with a combined record in Qualifications, Regional Pool Play, and Elimination Rounds of 17-0.
- Valley Sports pitcher Aaron Alvey **set the World Series record** for strikeouts (44), for consecutive scoreless innings pitched (21), and tied the record for consecutive no-hit innings pitched (12). Also, he **delivered the only run of the championship game** with a solo homerun in the top of the first inning. That team from Sendai, Japan was previously undefeated and had only allowed one run to score against its past five opponents combined.
- The Kentucky Colonels were a member of the American Basketball Association (ABA) for all nine years of its existence (1967-1976).
- The Colonels **won more games** than any other ABA franchise: 448 regular season games and 55 playoff games.
- The Colonels **won the ABA Championship** in 1974-75, going 12-3 in the playoffs. It was rumored (and reported) that John Y. Brown, as owner of the champion Colonels, offered one million dollars to the NBA champion Golden State Warriors to play a single game for the world title, **but they refused to play**.
- After the 1975-76 season, the NBA added four teams from the ABA and the Colonels were left out even though they were the **winningest ABA franchise** and also had a winning overall record (in exhibition games) against the NBA. Louisville has not had a major pro sports franchise ever since.

Homegrown Nicknames of Greatness

- **"Golden Boy"**: Paul Hornung won the Heisman Trophy with Notre Dame in 1956 and became the top overall pick in the NFL draft, an NFL Most Valuable Player, and 4-time NFL champion. Born and raised in Louisville, he set the all-time record for points scored in a 12-game season (176 points) with the Green Bay Packers in 1960.

- **"Madame Butterfly"**: Mary T. Meagher became a 3-time gold medal winning swimmer at the 1984 Olympics in Los Angeles after missing her chance to dominate the 1980 Olympics in Moscow due to the US boycott. She set 7 world records from her origins in Louisville, KY.

- **"Dr. Dunkenstein"**: Darrell Griffith won the John Wooden Award in 1980 as the best player in Men's College Basketball after leading UofL to its first national title - which he predicted upon signing with his hometown team out of local Male High School. He was the #2 pick in the 1980 NBA draft, won NBA Rookie of the Year, and set an NBA record for most 3-pointers made in a season in 1984, while leading the league in 3-point %.

- **"The Louisville Lip"**: Muhammad Ali was a Gold-medal winner and 3-time world heavyweight boxing champion born and raised in Louisville, KY. He has a few other nicknames, including "The People's Champion," and of course…
"The Greatest."

Born or Raised in Louisville

⚜ Wes Unseld, born and raised in Louisville, was a 2-time state basketball champion at Seneca H.S., averaged 23 points and 20 rebounds per game throughout his 4 years at UofL (including 36ppg and 24 rpg on the freshman team) while becoming a 2-time All American, was the #2 draft pick of the Baltimore Bullets in 1968, is one of only 2 players to ever win the NBA Rookie of the Year and Most Valuable Player Awards in the same season (Wilt Chamberlain is the other), was NBA Champion and Finals MVP in 1978, was inducted into the Naismith Memorial Basketball Hall of Fame in 1988, and voted one of The 50 Greatest Players in NBA History in 1998.

⚜ Pee Wee Reese was born in Ekron, KY and moved to Louisville at age 7. Nicknamed "The Little Colonel," Reese played 16 seasons as shortstop for the Brooklyn Dodgers, and was a Major League All Star ten consecutive seasons. He had his #1 jersey retired by the Dodgers in 1984. More importantly, Reese played an integral role in breaking the color barrier in major league baseball in 1947. As the popular and respected captain of the Dodgers, he privately and publicly accepted and embraced Jackie Robinson as the league's first black player at a time when many fans (and players) did not. Sometimes, true greatness supersedes what happens when the ball is in play.

LOUIS XVI
1754 · 1793
KING OF FRANCE

Flashes of Greatness

- Former New York Giants quarterback Phil Simms was born in Springfield, KY, grew up in Louisville, and attended Southern High School. He had a marvelous NFL career highlighted by his MVP performance in Super Bowl XXI in which he **set a new record** for passing accuracy (22 of 25, with 3 touchdowns).

- Former UofL kicker David Akers **set several NFL records** including Most Consecutive FGs Made in the Playoffs (19) and longest non-altitude assisted FG in history (63 yards).

- Former UofL defensive tackle Amobi Okoye became the **youngest player ever** to be drafted in the first round of the NFL in 2007 at age 19.

- Former UofL defensive end Elvis Dumervil **set an NCAA record** for sacks in a game (6) vs. UK in 2005 and led the NFL in sacks in 2009.

- Louisville native Danny Sullivan **won the Indianapolis 500** in 1985.

- Louisville native Bobby Nichols **won the PGA Championship** in 1964.

- Former UofL women's basketball player Angel McCoughtry was the #1 pick in the 2009 WNBA draft and has already **led the league** in scoring and steals twice.

- Former UofL runner Wesley Korir **won the Boston Marathon** in 2012 with a time of 2:12:40, which translates into just over 5 minutes per mile – for 26.2 miles!

- Former UofL wide receiver Deion Branch ranks in the **top five all-time** for career receptions and yards in the Super Bowl (24 receptions for 321 yards in 3 appearances), earning MVP of the game in 2004. Branch twice caught ten or more passes in a Super Bowl. He is the **only player** besides Jerry Rice to ever accomplish that feat. Rice has been voted Greatest NFL Player of All Time, so Branch is definitely in the company of greatness.

Thank you!

This book was written by a fan, for the fans. In creating it, I visited the museums, walked on the fields, touched the court at the YUM Center, smelled the greens at Valhalla, wandered the backside at Churchill Downs, ran the steps at the Ali Center…and those experiences actually highlight the true meaning of this book. It is about Louisville. It is not about a few transcendent people or teams that rose to greatness from the same city, it is about the city itself.

There is definitely something very special about our city that we should all be proud of. There is an intangible greatness in the air here. There is something unique about Louisville that keeps so many Louisvillians here, that brings so many back if they leave, and that makes it so easy for newcomers to call home. Initially, this was just a passion project created by a guy who loves sports, and who loves this town. The response has been so overwhelming that I am beginning to think there should be a copy on every coffee table or man-cave in Louisville.

Of course this dream would not be possible without the enormous contributions of those featured throughout this book. So from all of us, to all of you, thank you for making Louisville the Greatest City in Sports.

An Apology and Two Calls to Action

- ⚜ I apologize for any omissions of Greatness from this book – there is no way to include them all. I tried to focus on greatness that was both uniquely great and uniquely tied to Louisville. I'm sure I missed more than a few, and I sincerely thank every single person who has contributed to the greatness of sports in our city, whether mentioned in this book or not.

- ⚜ If you don't already, please visit our museums and study the lives and stories of Louisville's undeniable greatness. Please pass that knowledge, passion, and respect on to the next generation.

- ⚜ And as for our next generation, I encourage you to honor our past and build on it with your own personal brand of greatness - whether in sports or any other endeavor. It has been proven beyond the shadow of a doubt that Louisville is the Greatest. Join in!

"One more thing…"

- The quote on the cover of this book was chosen very deliberately:

   "The challenger from Louisville, KY wearing white trunks with red stripes…"

   This is how Cassius Clay was introduced to the world by ring announcer Frank Freeman just before he won his first heavyweight title from Sonny Liston, as a massive 7-1 underdog. Ali knew he was the underdog. He also knew he was The Greatest. Louisville is still the underdog in many ways, but those of us who are really paying attention also know that *Louisville is The Greatest*.

- There are dozens of really great sports towns in America, and it was not my aim to diminish any of them. I simply set out to build the case that Louisville is The Greatest. You may disagree with this conclusion, but there is no doubt that Louisville is definitely in the conversation. I just wanted to start the conversation. And end it.

- Muhammad Ali fought Joe Frazier three times. They fought 41 rounds of the most intense heavyweight boxing you will ever see. Finally, when Frazier was unable to answer the bell to begin the 42nd round of this epic rivalry, the Louisville Lip was the victor. An exhausted Ali had barely made it to the center of the ring where he sat down and was immediately interviewed. He mentioned Louisville five times in that brief interview, closing it out with this powerful statement:

   **"One more thing. I want everybody to know that I'm the greatest fighter
   of all times and the greatest city of all times is Louisville, KY!"**

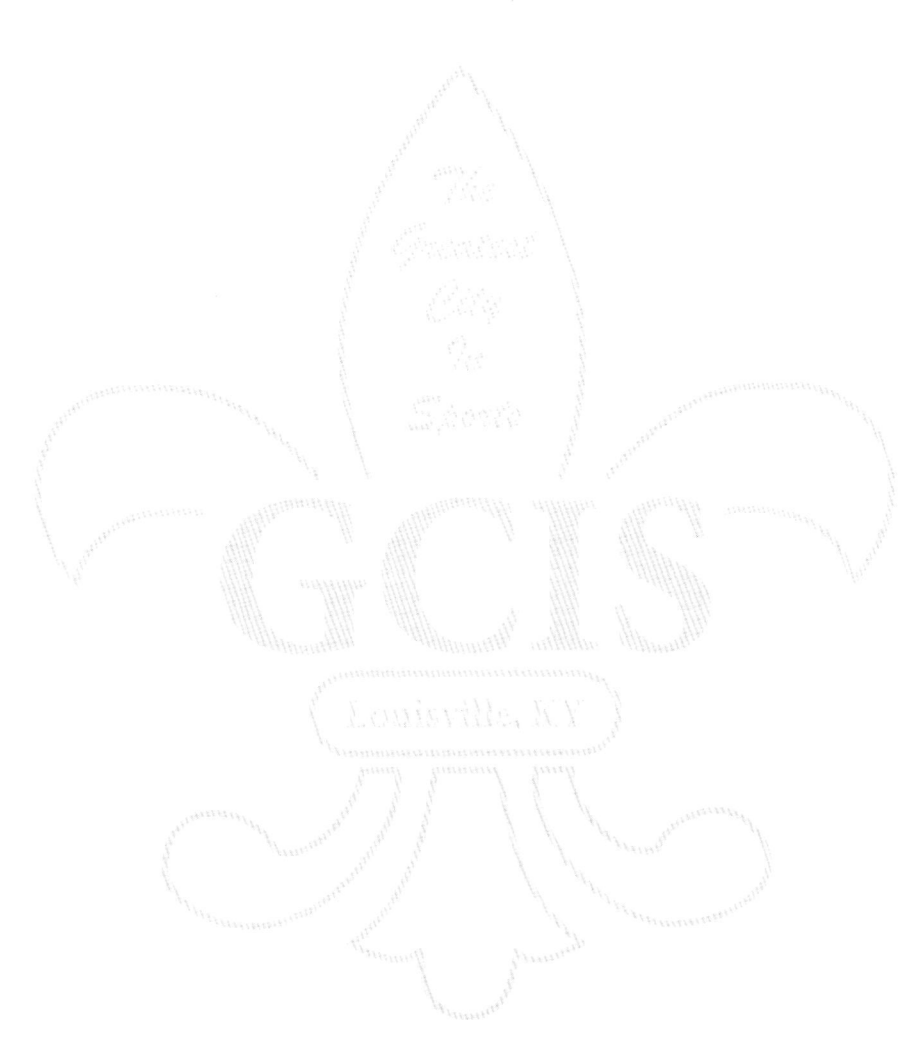

www.thegreatestcityinsports.com

Sources/References

Muhammad Ali Center: 144 North Sixth Street – Louisville, KY 40202

Kentucky Derby Museum: 704 Central Avenue – Louisville, KY 40208

Louisville Slugger Museum: 800 West Main Street – Louisville, KY 40202

Valhalla Golf Club: 15503 Shelbyville Road – Louisville, KY 40245

University of Louisville: 2301 South Third Street – Louisville, KY 40292

KFC YUM! Center: 1 Arena Plaza – Louisville, KY 40202

Papa Johns Cardinal Stadium: 2800 South Floyd Street – Louisville, KY 40209

Jim Patterson Stadium: 3015 South Third Street – Louisville, KY 40208

Louisville Slugger Field: 401 East Main Street – Louisville, KY 40202

Bellarmine University: 2001 Newburg Road – Louisville, KY 40205

Freedom Hall: 937 Phillips Lane – Louisville, KY 40209

https://espn.go.com/sportscentury/athletes.html
http://www.sportingnews.com/
http://www.sports-reference.com/
http://businessofcollegesports.com/2013/11/14/most-profitable-football-and-basketball-programs/
http://bleacherreport.com/articles/1128435-the-100-most-heated-rivalries-in-sports
https://scholarblogs.emory.edu/esma/2014/07/15/2014-college-basketball-fan-equity-rankings/
http://www.nba.com/history/players/50greatest.html
http://www.wsj.com/articles/the-college-basketball-capital-of-the-world-1425582625
*most college basketball stats are updated through the 2013-2014 tournament.